KWJC

W9-BJK-971

GYMNASTICS

BY KARA L. LAUGHLIN

Published by The Child's World®
1980 Lookout Drive • Mankato, MN 56003-1705
800-599-READ • www.childsworld.com

ACKNOWLEDGMENTS
The Child's World®: Mary Swensen, Publishing Director
The Design Lab: Design
Heidi Hogg: Editing
Sarah M. Miller: Editing

PHOTO CREDITS
© Air Images/Shutterstock.com: 20; Alex Emanuel Koch/
Shutterstock.com: 2-3; Aspen Photo/Shutterstock.com: 16;
Brendan Howard/Shutterstock.com: 19; Luigi Fardella/
Shutterstock.com: 15; Michael C. Gray/Shutterstock.com:
cover, 1; Nataliya Turpitko/Shutterstock.com: 4; Paolo Bona/
Shutterstock.com: 13; Sasha Samardzija/Shutterstock.com: 9;
tankist276/Shutterstock.com: 10; Valeria73/Shutterstock.com: 7

ISBN: 9781503807761
LCCN: 2015958124

Printed in the United States of America
Mankato, MN
June, 2016
PA02300

TABLE OF CONTENTS

4

Jump, Twist, and Spin

Do you love to roll down hills? Do you see a tree and think, "How would I climb that?" If so, you might be a gymnast.

In gymnastics, you move your body in daring ways. You fling yourself around high bars. You jump. You twist. You spin in the air.

Events

Every gymnastics team has six members. The team practices together. They help one another learn.

Boys compete in six events. Girls have four. Vault and floor are events for both. Girls also have beam and **uneven bars**. Boys have **rings**, **parallel bars**, **high bar**, and **horse**.

Vault

In the vault event, gymnasts run, jump, and push off the **vault table** into the air. They twist and flip before they land on the mat.

Fast Fact!
Some gymnasts call the vault table "the tongue" because of its shape.

10

Apparatus Art

In ring, horse, and bar events, gymnasts swing their bodies around an **apparatus**. Boys also do **holds**. During a hold, every part of your body must be still.

Fast Fact!
The horse is also called the pommel horse or the side horse.

11

Floor

For the floor event, gymnasts do strings of moves called **passes**. They run, jump, flip, and then flip again. The floor has springs under it and pads on top. That makes for high jumps and soft landings.

Beam

The beam event is a little like the floor event. Girls combine moves. They tumble and spin—but on a skinny beam instead. The beam is just four inches (10 centimeters) wide. Girls go slow and focus to keep from falling.

Fast Fact!
Gymnasts use chalk to keep their hands dry and help their grip.

Sticking It

Most events end with a tumble through the air. Gymnasts work hard to **stick** the landing. They land on both feet. They try not to take a step. If they do, they will get a lower score.

Scoring

Judges score each **routine**. For every error, they lower the score. If the moves are hard, the score will be higher.

Fast Fact!
Judges give more points for difficult moves. They also give more points when a gymnast uses great skill.

The best teams win medals. The boys and girls with the most points do, too. The medals are reminders of a day of courage and skill.

Fast Fact!
Shannon Miller has the most medals of any American gymnast.

Glossary

apparatus (ap-uh-RAT-uss): Any piece of gymnastics equipment used for an event is called an apparatus.

high bar (HY BAR): The high bar is a bar held about nine feet (3 meters) above the ground that boys swing on while doing a routine.

holds (HOLDS): When doing holds, every part of a gymnast's body must be still.

horse (HORSS): Boys use this apparatus with two handles to perform routines.

parallel bars (PAYR-uh-lel BARZ): Two long bars pointing in the same direction which boys swing over and around.

passes (PASS-ez): Passes are series of strung-together moves done one after the other during the floor exercise.

rings (RINGZ): Two rings hung in the air that boys must grasp during a routine. The rings are not supposed to swing or move during a routine.

routine (roo-TEEN): A planned series of moves that a gymnast performs during an event is called a routine.

stick (STIK): To land as if one's feet are stuck to the ground. Gymnasts want to stick their landings, because hops and steps after the landing will get them lower scores.

uneven bars (un-EE-ven BARZ): An apparatus with two bars that point in the same direction, with one lower and farther forward than the other.

vault table (VAHLT TAY-bul): A piece of equipment onto which gymnasts spring. They use the vault table to launch themselves high in the air, where they do a series of flips and twists before they land.

To Learn More

In the Library

Kawa, Katie. *The Science of Gymnastics*.
New York, NY: PowerKids Press, 2016.

Savage, Jeff. *Top 25 Gymnastics Skills, Tips, and Tricks*.
Berkeley Heights, NJ: Enslow Publishers, 2012.

Schlegel, Elfi, and Claire Ross Dunn. *The Gymnastics Book: The Young Performer's Guide to Gymnastics*.
Richmond Hill, Ont.: Firefly Books, 2012.

On the Web

Visit our Web site for links about gymnastics:
childsworld.com/links

Note to Parents, Teachers, and Librarians: We routinely verify
our Web links to make sure they are safe and active sites.
So encourage your readers to check them out!

Index

About the Author

Kara L. Laughlin is an artist and writer who lives in Virginia with her husband, three kids, two guinea pigs, and a dog. She is the author of two dozen nonfiction books for kids.